REAL ESTATE
IN
PANAMA!

Don't miss your portion!

ACKNOWLEDGMENTS

To God, to me and to my family.

COPYRIGHTS ®

The total or partial reproduction of this work by any means or procedure, whether electronic or mechanical, computer processing, rental, or any other form of transfer of rights is prohibited, without the prior written authorization of the copyright holder.

Real estate in Panama

2nd EDITION, Jul 2025

All rights reserved Marina Chu L. © Panama

1st Edition August 2024.

INTRODUCTION

Real estate is a long-term investment tool, a refuge for capital in uncertain times, an investment if we do our homework well. Learn a little about the real estate market in Panama and its value for investing.

This book is a basic guide for those seeking to navigate the Panamanian real estate market. It was written by a Panamanian and aims to review the relevant aspects involved when considering the purchase of a home in Panama, for both nationals and foreigners, taking into account important aspects that go beyond just a good location.

Important topics related to the real estate brokerage profession and existing regulation are also explored.

Panama is on fashion!

INDEX

CHAPTER I 13
Why Panama? 13
   1.1. Economy 13
   1.2. Security and absence of natural cataclysms. 16
   1.3. Excellent connectivity over the air 18
   1.4. Political stability, dollarized economy, international banking center. 18
   1.5. Favorite destination for retirees 20
CHAPTER 2 23
Real estate as an investment 23
   2.1. Property valuation 23
   2.2. ROI 26
   2.3. Real estate as the best refuge of value in uncertain times. 27
   2.4. Panama as a recognized real estate destination 29
CHAPTER 3 31
Development of the Panamanian real estate market. 31
   3.1. Panama after December 20, 1989 31
   3.2. Last 10 years in the construction sector 32
   3.3. Incentives for the construction of housing solutions 33
   3.4. Panama Real Estate Outlook 2024 36
CHAPTER 4 37
Understanding a little, the real estate market in Panama. 37
   4.1. Demand characteristics 37
   4.2. Features of the offer 38
   4.3. Profile of the buyers 40

4.4. Profile of the sellers 43

4.5. Services offered by real estate brokers or real estate agents 46

CHAPTER 5 49

The Panamanian banking system and mortgage loans. 49

5.1. Mortgage portfolio details: 49

5.2. Bank requirements to apply for mortgage loans. 51

5.3. Prime interest rates and other interest rates 52

5.4. Growth of the mortgage loan portfolio of Panamanian banks 53

CHAPTER 6 55

Choosing your first home (what to consider?) 55

6.1. As a single person 55

6.2. As a married, in free union 58

6.3. Investment (rent) 59

6.4. Doing   numbers! 60

CHAPTER 7 63

I have a property and now what? 63

7.1. Protect your investment 63

7.1.1. Annual maintenance 63

7.1.2. Location appreciation 63

7.1.2. ¿Do improvements increase value? 71

7.1.3. Improve loan rates, shorten mortgage time. 74

7.2. Invest in a second home. 76

7.2.1. Use of the second home 76

7.2.2. How will it be paid? 77

7.2.3. Have a plan for the use of the home, when it is not being used. 80

7.2.4. Sharing property with another person, sharing benefits and responsibilities. 81

7.2.5. Use your home as leverage to invest. 82

7.3. Register your main home as family assets with the DGI ("Direcciòn General de Ingresos") 82

CHAPTER 8 85

I want to be a Real Estate Broker, Real Estate Agent, Property Manager, or whatever it's called! 85

8.1. Real Estate Broker License Requirements 85

8.1.1. Natural Person Requirements: 86

8.1.2. Legal Entity Requirements: 87

8.2. To manage his license: 88

8.3. Legal Framework 88

8.4. Registration for the Real Estate Broker License Exam . 89

8.4.1. National Person (natural or legal) 89

8.4.2. Foreign Person 90

8.5. Procedure for taking the exam 90

8.6. Requirements to obtain the Real Estate Certification. ... 91

8.7. Syllabus for the exam 92

8.7.1. Laws and regulations of the Real Estate Technical Board. 92

8.7.2. Prevention of money laundering: 93

8.7.3. Contracts 95

8.7.4. Lease 96

8.7.5. Urban Planning and Zoning 96

8.7.6. State and island lands/" Casco Antiguo" or old town 97

8.7.7. Taxes and Credit Banking 98

8.7.8. Free Zones 99

- 8.7.9. Other Laws 100
- 8.8. Solving conflicts 100
- CHAPTER 9 103
- Know and understand the profession. 103
  - 9.1. The vocation of service and ethics. 103
  - 9.2. Make yourself known. 104
  - 9.3. Work alone, with partners, or under international representation. 105
    - 9.3.1. Work individually: 106
    - 9.3.2. Work with partners: 106
    - 9.3.3. under a representation international 107
- CHAPTER 10 109
- Grow or stagnate in times of inflation! 109
  - 10.1. About real estate bubbles and other demons. 109
  - 10.2. Excess supply and demand restricted by high interest rates. 110
  - 10.3. "Staying alive" 112
  - **BIBLIOGRAPHY** 119

CHAPTER I

Why Panama?

1.1. Economy

Panama's economy is one of the most stable on the continent. Among its main economic activities are logistics, tourism, and financial services. These three activities represent a total of 75% of its GDP.

Panama is a country of services, currently the largest exporter in Central America of financial, logistics, and telecommunications services.

Having all the potential to be the Singapore of America, Panama has a conglomerate of transportation and logistics services oriented towards global trade, whose nerve center is the Panama Canal. Around it, there are container transshipment ports, free trade zones, a railway and the largest air passenger hub in Latin America.

Its financial center is the largest in Latin America. The network of services it offers is well interconnected with the world market. These services account for around three quarters of its GDP.

In recent years, the construction of skyscrapers has been notable in Panama City and has grown rapidly because of several aspects, among which stand out sustainable and consecutive economic growth for 20 years since 1989; government support with interest rate subsidies for the acquisition of a first home; and a high demand for affordable housing solutions.

The tourism sector has also been booming because of the creation and constant expansion of the region's air hub, which has had the capacity to move passengers from any origin in Latin America to Panama and from Panama to any destination in the region.

Investment in Panama has become the main drivers of GDP growth in recent years. Since 2004, investment has exceeded $1 billion, a record for the country; From there it has been leading the Central American region in terms of investment amount and ranks second in foreign investment per capita in Latin America, after Chile.

Panama is one of the few countries in the region in which its growth rate has remained stable and constant, except in the recent period of the Covid.19 Pandemic, where, like the rest of the planet, it experienced a forced pause.

Figure 1

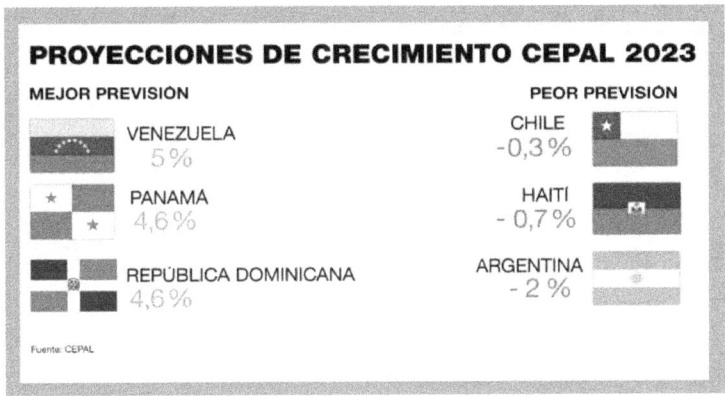

SOURCE: ECLAC. GDP growth projection for 2023 in some countries in Latin America.

The Panamanian economy is the tenth economy in Latin America in terms of nominal GDP (exceeding Costa Rica and Ecuador) and the eleventh in terms of GDP at purchasing power parity (PPP) prices (after Guatemala and before Costa Rica). Panama has a per capita income of USD 11,849 nominal and USD 20,512 PPP.

It should be noted that from 2003 to 2009, Panama's GDP doubled. According to the World Bank, the IMF and the UN, the country has the highest per capita income in Central America, which is about 13,090 US dollars. One fact to highlight is that the GDP has grown steadily for more than twenty consecutive years. Just after the North American invasion in December 1989, of which it was subjected, and which subsequently resulted in the flourishing of its economy.

An average economic growth of 8% has been maintained in the last 10 years and the GDP growth outlook for the coming years is between 4.6 and 6% annually. However, with the wars in Ukraine and the Gaza Strip, the economy in general has been greatly affected around the world as they are directly linked to the costs of raw materials, oil and agricultural inputs, among other important variables. Due to the above, Panama's growth forecast will most likely not exceed 3-4% in the coming years, on a speculative basis.

In a global economy, constantly influenced by variables that are beyond human control, such as pandemics, wars, climate change, natural disasters, it is increasingly essential to have haven economies to invest in. Panama has all the necessary characteristics to be identified as a place where investments are safe, let's continue reviewing them.

1.2. Security and absence of natural cataclysms.

Panama appears in the safety rankings, as one of the safest countries in Latin America to travel and live. However, as everywhere, safety measures and common sense must be kept in mind. The first security barrier begins with us.

According to the Crime Index by Country 2023 from Numbeo (a website that compiles data contributions from countries), Panama has a percentage of 56.32%. Costa Rica and the United States have safety rates of 46.3% and 50.98% respectively. This indicates that Panama is a relatively safe country.

When a tourist or foreigner residing in Panama is asked what they like most about visiting or living in Panama, they usually answer that they like the feeling of security very much. They also really like the idiosyncrasy of the Panamanian, which is a peaceful character and open doors to new cultures.

Due to its privileged geographical position, Panama is protected from extreme tropical storms. Furthermore, there have been no large earthquakes recorded in recent years that have caused serious structural damage or numerous human losses.

1.3. Excellent connectivity over the air

Due to its central position on the world map, and the sustained expansion of the air hub, it has excellent connections with Europe, Asia and America. Panama is among the countries that have already managed to recover the passenger air traffic that was recorded in 2019, prior to the Covid Pandemic. This is an indicator that Panama's efficient interconnectivity meets all the standards required by the international market.

It is estimated that the Tocumen International Airport could have a passenger movement of more than 17 million per year. The renowned Panamanian airline COPA has its operations center in Panama, which constitutes connectivity security in the region.

1.4. Political stability, dollarized economy, international banking center.

Since the invasion of Panama by US military forces in 1989, the country has enjoyed complete democracy. Since then, presidential elections have been held that have received the support and recognition of the international community.

This has created a suitable climate for important infrastructure projects to be carried out, for example, the construction of the third set of locks of its interoceanic canal.

The Republic of Panama declared the US dollar its official currency in 1904 as an economic guarantee for the United States on the construction of the Panama Canal. From that moment on, the US dollar has "par value" with the Balboa, the official currency. This fact has represented undeniable support for the economy, being an outstanding advantage to stimulate its economic activities (thus avoiding monetary and balance of payments crises).

The banking center of Panama is mainly made up of private banks with international capital. During the last 30 years, it has consolidated itself as one of the most important international financial centers in Latin America, due to its legislation to establish itself; promotion by government; geographical location with respect to the region; its relative economic and political stability and dollarization of its economy.

On July 8, 1941, Law 101 was issued, through which banking activity in Panama was regulated, appointing the

Ministry of Finance and Treasury (today known as the Ministry of Economy and Finance) in charge of controlling the banking system and Comptroller General of the Republic of the supervision of this. Despite this, the activity grew rapidly and with little control, so the government sector had to adopt legal measures to exercise better control and avoid foreseeable inconveniences, approving Cabinet Decree No. 238 dated July 2, 1970, establishing the first banking law that creates the National Banking Commission, as an entity that promotes banking activity in Panama.

The 1970 Law allowed the development of the International Banking Center, promoting the arrival of several investment banks. It is for this reason that the International Banking Center of Panama has become one of the main ones in Latin America.

After the creation of the 1970 Law, on February 26, 1998, a regulatory authority for banking activity was established in Panama, creating the Superintendency of Banks.

1.5. Favorite destination for retirees

After a lifetime dedicated to work, when retirement arrives, one aspires to abandon the slavery of schedules and be able to enjoy peaceful, interesting and economically convenient places that provide housing, food, transportation, medical care and entertainment facilities to a reasonable cost.

Panama is not considered anymore "the best kept secret". Every year, the Central American country appears on lists of the best destinations to consider retiring. Furthermore, thanks to the boost in air interconnectivity offered by its hub, named "hub of the Americas" located at the Tocumen International Airport, Panama is increasingly presenting itself as an offer in investment, tourism, and a place of permanent residence or second residence.

Due to its quality of life, security levels, moderate housing costs, special discounts for retirees, entertainment offers, among other advantages, Panama continues to receive retirees who want to take advantage of their retirement with a better quality-cost ratio. Canada and the United States are among the main countries from which retired immigrants are received.

Panama is cheaper, at least, than Costa Rica, Uruguay, and Mexico to retire to. Increasingly, it is important that retirement has and sustains the quality of life required in the golden years, the average life expectancy is around 75-80 years, and it is no longer so unusual to find people over 90 and even 100 years old.

"Real estate tourism" has emerged as other reasons to go to Panama. The attractions it offers in terms of its real estate offering, backed by an international banking center, make it a market comparable to Miami, in United States.

In Panama it is also possible to invest and obtain residency with the purchase of real estate.

CHAPTER 2

Real estate as an investment

2.1. Property valuation

For the purposes of clarity, this book's focus is investment in residential real estate. Focusing on the acquisition of the first home and for an individual.

Based on the above, in general terms, a property or real estate is valued considering the following factors:

a. Environment and location: the city, township, neighborhood, what type of businesses are nearby, security, access to public transportation, among the main things, will determine the value of a property in the first instance. As they say: "location, location, location".

b. Topography: a detailed study of the surface of the land, which includes changes in the surface, such as mountains and valleys, as well as the characteristics of existing rivers and roads, is essential. However, this detail is taken more into account when considering the purchase of land for commercial development. In the case of a home, whether called a house or apartment, it can be summarized by investigating the possible threats of flooding, due to the proximity of rivers, streams or stagnant waters. Sadly, in Panama, there have been several cases of entire neighborhoods built in unsafe places with river overflows.

c. Construction: quality of materials, execution of the work in terms of design, which influence the appearance and may determine its appreciation or devaluation. In Panama, the issue of inspecting whether the property has cracks, lifting of floors, water leaks, or excessive humidity that favors the presence of mold is highlighted.

d. Physical attributes of the property: finishes, special characteristics, appearance of the property. The set of these points will answer the questions of:

- What is the impression we receive when we visit it? (if it is already built)

- What is the impression we want to transmit or receive? (if the home is under construction planning)

e. Legal issues of the property: if it has pending issues such as payment of taxes, updating of cadastral value, seizure, mortgages. Additionally, the property must be correctly verified in its location, dimensions and ownership.

f. Supply and demand: the real estate market, like any other market, can be positive for buyers or sellers, as well as present a good balance for both, it is important to be aware of this and do not have false expectations.

g. Economic news of the region or country: unemployment, high interest rates (inflationary economies), changing mortgage loans requirements, high costs in construction industry (labor and materials), influence directly. In Panama, the significant increase in materials and labor is already fully reflected in prices. Additionally, the constant demand for housing solutions, especially in key areas of Panama City, means that a downward adjustment in prices is not in sight.

2.2. ROI

Panama is today a valuable real estate market for buying, selling or renting. Expats from all over the world are sent to Panama to work in multinational companies. Many of them decide to invest in one or more properties. It is important to highlight that foreigner, through the purchase of real estate, receive the opportunity to acquire residence in a country considered a first-class financial and tourist center.

The reality is that investing in a property in Panama can has a ROI (return on investment) of 5% to 9% in rental income. Keep in mind that the valuation factors previously reviewed must be considered.

The real estate market is a great opportunity to work sustainably and safely on a family asset or investment portfolio, so that, when renting, in addition to "paying for the property alone," there is still an attractive benefit.

The country is seen as a growing, maturing and evolving real estate market. In addition to being in a first-world business center, with a high quality of life, it is also considered a reference for investments. Also of interest is the new legislation that allows to acquire permanent residence in Panama, through the acquisition of real estate, if you deposit the entire amount of the property's value in a trust.

2.3. Real estate as the best refuge of value in uncertain times.

At the end of 2020 and beginning of 2021, a phenomenon was detected during the COVID-19 pandemic in many countries around the world, which industry experts called the "real estate boom." In Panama, "book value" or appreciation, year after year, is 5%, so it is an important percentage to consider when choosing a real estate market to invest in. This is a percentage established as a valuation reference by the competent authority. However, this is not guaranteed and will depend on the valuation factors to be considered in a property.

Owning various properties is not only a long-term investment since it is also increasing the value of family assets or investment portfolios. It means that real estate continues to increase in value for a long time, until it is decided to sell it to make a new real estate investment or another investment.

Two investments tools that investors choose to constantly discuss are real estate and the stock market.

Let's do an exercise on the level of risk in real estate and the stock market:

Figure 2

	Real Estate	**Stock Market**
Accumulated value	low	low
Control	low	MEDIUM
Liquidity	MEDIUM	MEDIUM
Stability	low	HIGH

Risk between Real Estate and Stock Market. Source: own

Of course, it is assumed that each case and scenario must be analyzed, in short, investment in real estate, at least in Panama, if all the tasks have been done, represents a low risk in general, considering in these moments of high inflation and high mortgage interest rates.

2.4. Panama as a recognized real estate destination

Before describing Panama, as a real estate destination, let's do a rough review of the region, starting with Costa Rica, known as a destination for retirees, for tourists who seek relaxation near nature, very famous among film artists. and investors, however, suffers from overvaluation. Currently, Costa Rica is the most expensive country to live in the region.

Finally, Guatemala, Honduras, El Salvador and Nicaragua experience constant political and economic ups and downs that make them very insecure for a long-term investment plan.

Due to the above, Panama stands out as a unique opportunity in the region, as it has important characteristics that make it ideal for investors. In all Latin America, there is not a country with so many competitive advantages to be able to invest in real estate. It is more diverse, modern, less expensive than Costa Rica, it is more economically and politically stable than the rest of its Central American neighbors, and it also has an excellent score on security issues.

Panama has high connectivity due to its geographical position, its local currency, the Balboa, has par value with the US dollar, and it has an international financial center that offers highly competitive and business-oriented services in the region.

Panama is politically stable and has sustained economic development growth, averaging between 4-6% year after year. However, with the result of the recent presidential elections held in May 2024, a period of adaptation of the economy to possible new economic policies is expected. As consequence, this may lead the market to rethink the GDP growth.

CHAPTER 3

Development of the Panamanian real estate market.

3.1. Panama after December 20, 1989

After the social-political crisis and US invasion of Panama, at the beginning of the 90s, Panama had a gross domestic product (nominal) of USD 5,632 million. By 1999, the country's GDP reached USD 12.13 billion. The Panamanian economy had a growth of 115.3% during this decade compared to the GDP of 1990. This was an incredible exponential leap, demonstrating the great potential of the economy, subject to political restrictions that affected its growth.

Figure 3

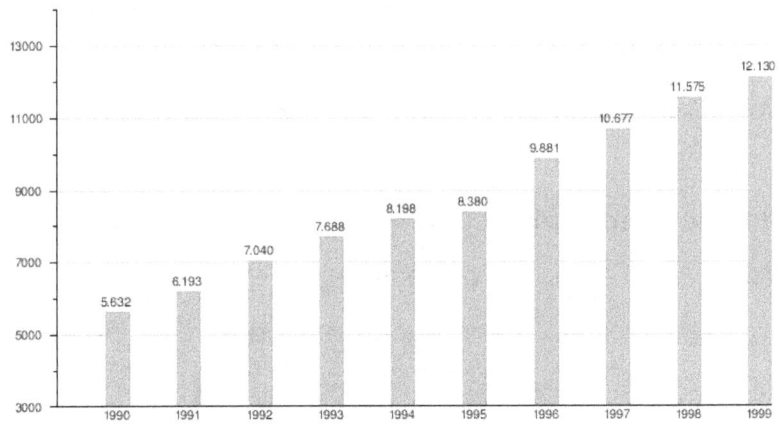

Panama GDP growth 1990-1999
Source: International Monetary Fund

This dynamism in the economy involved the construction sector, as we will see below.

3.2. Last 10 years in the construction sector

Every year the construction sector has had an important participation in the GDP. In the last 10 years, its peak year, was 2015 when it reached an unprecedented boom that finally took off the sector that had already been demonstrating an outstanding participation in economic development.

Until 2019, the participation of the Construction sector in Panama represented 16.2% of the Gross Domestic Product (GDP). As expected, like the rest of the economy, the Construction sector paralyzed its activities, to give priority to the national and global health emergency of Covid.19.

The pandemic marked an extreme contraction in the growth and evolution of construction. From August 2019 to September 2020, the sector ranked third in job losses with 34,148. However, in 2022, the Construction sector grew by 9%, reported the Minister of Economy and Finance, Hector Alexander.

"This sector gives life to other activities related to the industry and directly benefits thousands of people who work in it," he said when approached by journalists at the inauguration of the Expo Acobir Real Estate 2023.

Hector Alexander also added that many households depend directly and indirectly on construction and the behavior of the real estate market, which has led to Panama's economic recovery, being one of the clearest in the hemisphere.

3.3. Incentives for the construction of housing solutions

As a timely update, a new law is now in place regarding preferential interest rates for first-time homeowners purchased by Panamanians and foreigners with permanent residence.

Law 468 of April 24, 2025, supersedes Law 3 of 1985, which established a preferential interest rate regime, and establishes other provisions.

Upon the entry into force of this law, three preferential interest rate brackets are defined, divided into Region 1

(Panama and Western Panama) and Region 2 for the rest of the country.

Preferential Bracket No. 1, provides a maximum subsidized rate of 5.0%, for a non-renewable eight-year term, for preferential mortgage loans for the purchase of new homes with a purchase price of up to $50,000.00 at the time of financing.

Regarding Preferential Tranche No. 2, a maximum subsidized rate of 4.5% is established, for a non-renewable term of seven years, for preferential mortgage loans intended for the purchase of new homes, whose purchase price, at the time of financing, is between $50,000 and $80,000.

Meanwhile, Preferential Tranche No. 3, creates a maximum subsidized rate of 4.0%, for a non-renewable five-year term, for preferential mortgage loans for the purchase of new homes, with a purchase price at the time of financing of $80,000.1 cent and up to $120,000.

Similarly, the new law establishes, in its first article, that the established tax regime will apply to financial intermediaries, both public and private, duly authorized by the Superintendency of Banks of Panama, the National Banking Commission, or their corresponding regulatory body.

Important: At the recommendation of market stakeholders, the President of the Republic, José Raúl Mulino, signed Law 472, which reestablishes the preferential interest rate regime for mortgage loans established in Law 3 of 1985 until December 31, 2025, and allows banking institutions to continue processing mortgages currently in process.

This postpones the entry into force of Law 468 of 2025, which establishes new conditions for preferential interest rates, until January 1, 2026.

The President's approval establishes modifications to the current regulations on the Preferential Interest Rate Regime for Housing, making its implementation clearer, more orderly, and fairer. By temporarily suspending the entry into force of Law 468 of 2025, a more equitable transition is consolidated, without affecting the commitments made or the legitimate aspiration of families to own their own homes.

3.4. Panama Real Estate Outlook 2024

Inflation, high loan rates, high supply, low demand = slow market. The Panamanian real estate market is in a slow motion, almost in a scenario were buying and selling activity moves very slowly and at an almost incipient pace. We are in an elections year, traditionally, the economy in general tends to take its "precautions" in presidential election years, since it is known that each government comes with its own agenda under its arm, appropriate to the economic policies of the party that it be elected.

The figures that appeared at the beginning of 2024 place Panama's GDP growth at 4%, although quite moderate for recent years rates. The unemployment rate is 7.5% - 10%, as estimated by experts, however, there are no official government figures. These percentages are not a cause for major concern, but the government that is elected and its policies. Consumer confidence is important, without economic growth and without employment, it is difficult to stimulate it.

CHAPTER 4

Understanding a little, the real estate market in Panama.

4.1. Demand characteristics

Wisely, someone once said, that in real estate, the main thing to ensure was "location, location, location." Ask yourself if you would like to live in a palace, in the middle of nowhere?

It is notorious, the incessant demand for properties of differentiated quality in central areas of the capital city, such as San Francisco, Costa del Este, Avenida Balboa, Bella Vista, El Cangrejo, Santa María, Marbella. The real estate investment focuses, in addition to the location, on the search for a current and convenient lifestyle.

The characteristics of residential properties revolves around a lifestyle adapted to the post-Covid19 pandemic, since they are expected to have open spaces, to even have offices or work centers, and to be easy for technological adaptation. Of course, if you have the desired location, everything else will follow. The convenience of having nearby banks, pharmacies, hospitals, schools, parks for children and adults to play and exercise outdoors, all surrounded by a controlled and safe environment.

We live in times in which the pressure to be environmentally friendly is real. Buyers, in addition to having the comforts of the modern world, seek to have devices or options that contribute to efficiency in energy consumption in their homes.

In Panama, the demand for workspaces, or what we know as offices, is also characterized by the search for convenience, strategic location, modernly equipped that promote creativity, innovation and recreate a "coworking" environment.

4.2. Features of the offer

In Panama, the real estate offer, which are convenient either to invest as a first home, or to rent and have it as a long-term investment, is wide and varied. The investment amount of the real estate supply represents approximately 10% of the GDP, being an important percentage if it is considered that the annual GDP of Panama was $79,443 million US dollars in the year 2022, with a constant growth of at least 5% year after year.

Prime rate is the driving force of the real estate business in our country. In 2019, took place reforms that allowed to increase first home value, to apply for prime rate. With this action, the government promoted sales of homes whose value amounted to $180,000.00, being the maximum value to obtain a prime rate on mortgage loans.

In the years prior to 2019, home sales generated at least $640.1 million annually. 11.3% of the houses sold in 2022 were of social interest, which benefit from a solidarity bonus of $10 thousand and are exempt from the payment of bank interest. Contrasting the difference in percentages, 70.7% of real estate sales were made by middle class people, with the ability to pay bills ranging from $400 to $1000, and even more. Homes that had a value cap of $180,000.00 had a preferential interest between 1.5% and 4%.

The construction of real estate assets in strategic locations are mainly in: Marbella, Punta Paitilla, Punta Pacifica, Bella Vista, Obarrio, San Francisco, Altos del Golf, Coco del Mar, Avenida Balboa, Casco Antiguo, Santa María, El Cangrejo and Costa del Este. In the suburbs of the Panama City, there are also comfortable residential areas such as Albrook and Clayton.

With the above, it is concluded that the real estate offer in Panama City is limited to first-class, high-cost housing, with very few solutions in social housing that are functional and that inspire confidence.

4.3. Profile of the buyers

In Panama, the profile of buyers corresponds primarily to those looking to purchase their first home, whether as a single, engaged or married person. This is the case of a person or couple, with a good credit history, credit capacity in their salaries or income. The average age at the acquisition of the first home has been rising in recent years due to several factors, including lack of job stability, lack of credit capacity, engaging in so-called bad debts or credit cards and car purchases.

Another factor is the lack of formal employment, which is why credit institutions do not approve loans to people or couples who do not have job stability. It could almost be stated that the average age for purchasing the first home is around 37-40 years, complicating the planning of a retirement free of home loans.

Then we have real estate investors, among these are nationals and foreigners. They can be natural or legal persons. A bank or credit entity request from a Panamanian company or person about the same to approve loans, there are differences in the interest rates on the mortgage loan, duration of the loan granted and the percentage to be financed.

In Panama, foreign investment in real estate is quite notorious, there is what is known as a residence permit due to real estate investment. With a minimum amount of USD 300,000.00 in real estate, if it is proven that the funds come from abroad, it is possible to obtain a residence permit for a period of two (2) years, after this period the applicant may apply for the permanent residence.

Below are the requirements to apply for a residence permit, through investment in real estate:

1. Power of Attorney and Request (authenticated by a Notary Public).
2. Three (3) pictures.
3. Duly verified copy of the passport (authenticated by a Notary or corresponding Authority).
4. Criminal Record Certificate authenticated by Apostille

5. Health Certificate
6. Certified Check for USD 250.00 in favor of the National Treasury.
7. Certified Check for USD 800.00 in favor of the National Immigration Service.
8. Affidavit of Criminal record Form.
9. Certification from the Public Registry that proves the ownership of real estate (applicants name), with a minimum value of three hundred thousand (USD 300,000.00). The certification must indicate that the property is free of liens.
10. If the applicant has dependents, they must present the following:

    a. Responsibility letter.
    b. Proof of relationship.
    c. Proof of address.
    d. Over 18 years of age, present a certificate of single status and certified studies.

11. After the 2-year period has passed, you can apply for permanent residence, so the same previous requirements must be submitted except for the Criminal Record Certificate and the checks.

Additionally, you must present Income Tax Good Standing certificate.

4.4. Profile of the sellers

In Panama, a property can be sold directly by the owner (pre-owned homes), through a construction or development company (new projects), or through a broker. Brokers, or real estate agents, can be legal entities or individuals.

As of January 31, 2024, there were 1,462 real estate agent legal entities registered with the Real Estate Technical Board; however, several of them have had their license canceled or suspended. On the other hand, there are also 5,685 natural real estate agents, some of whom also have their license canceled or suspended. It is important that before agreeing to be seen by a real estate agent, you verify if she has a valid license. In Panama, it is illegal to carry out real estate transactions, on a commercial level, without having a valid license as a Real Estate Broker. You can check the status at the following link:
https://mici.gob.pa/jtbr-corredores-de-bienes-raices-idoneos/

In total, there are more than 7,000 real estate agents in Panama, who are there to advise on the sale of real estate offers, which total 39,879, as detailed below:

FIGURE 5

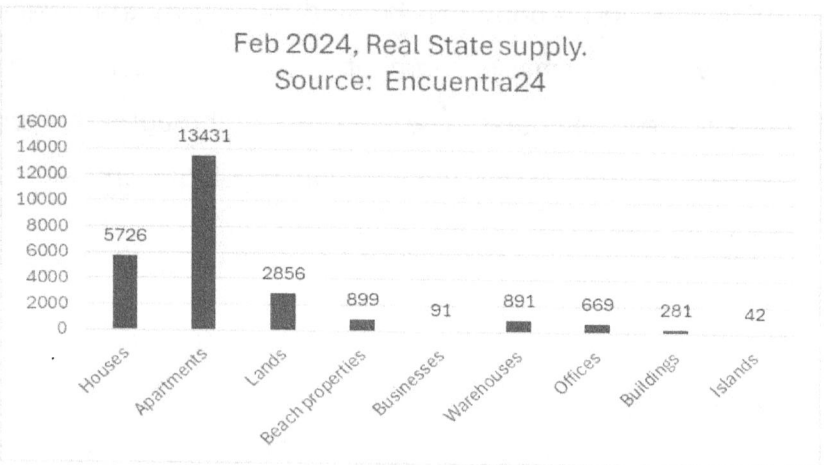

Feb 2024, Real State supply.
Source: Encuentra24

From this data, the apartments double the supply of houses.

During the year, in Panama City, several real estate fairs are organized. Credit entities offer mortgage loans, and all types of companies provide different complementary services.

The main real state fairs are:

- ACOBIR Real Estate Expo: organized every year by the Association of Real Estate Brokers and Developers, a pioneer in this type of fairs, ACOBIR every year promotes all the most important existing housing projects, throughout the national territory. In 2024, it took place at the Panama Convention Center, from January 25 to 28, with the participation of more than 100 exhibitors and more than 250 projects.

- CAPAC Housing Expo: organized by the Panamanian Chamber of Construction, in 2024, had its version from April 18 to 21. At this fair, the main national projects are exhibited and real estate agents, as well as developers of housing solutions, actively participate with stands.

- Expo Habitat: also organized by the Panamanian Chamber of Construction. In its 2023 version, it condensed 250 housing projects from 70 development companies and had the presence of service and goods companies. It is distinguished by the universality of its concept and the products on display. In addition, companies from countries in America, Asia and Europe participate that see Panama as an excellent opportunity for investment. The appointment in 2024, for this fair, is from September 5 to 8.

- FIPA real estate fair: this fair is focused on the real estate market for the middle and upper class. Likewise, Panama can offer housing solutions with differentiated and luxurious comfort. Its latest version, for which information is accessible, was developed in 2019, from August 4 to 5, at the Hotel Riu Convention room in Panama City.

4.5. Services offered by real estate brokers or real estate agents

Real estate agents mainly bring buyers and sellers together and vice versa. Although it is completely possible to carry out transactions directly (from seller to buyer), it is not advisable, since, during the transaction, problems may arise from one party or another, and it is very important that there is an expert intermediation that avoid conflicts and, above all, ensure a fair and secure transaction that meets the expectations of both parties.

The services provided by real estate agents or real estate brokers, are mainly the following:

- To promote sales through a website, offering a database open to interested parties.

- To answer questions to potential buyers.
- To show and display the promoted real estate assets.
- To prepare, if necessary, the documents to carry out the sale.
- To obtain information on mortgage financing for the interested party, who requests it.
- To investigate the status of the real estate in the Public Registry and the General Directorate of Revenue, to know the ownership, location, and description data, as well as the existence of liens, and tax debt.
- To serve as intermediaries between buyer and seller and maintain harmony and transparency in the transaction.

CHAPTER 5

The Panamanian banking system and mortgage loans.

5.1. Mortgage portfolio details:

FIGURE 6

SISTEMA BANCARIO NACIONAL
SALDO DE CREDITOS HIPOTECARIOS LOCALES
NOVIEMBRE 2023
(En Miles de Balboas)

	Bancos	PRESTAMO LOCAL	CREDITO HIPOTECARIO	PONDERACION (%)	VIVIENDA PROPIA	LOCAL COMERCIAL
1	Banco General, S.A.	10,549,565	4,454,846	42.23%	4,329,393	125,453
2	Caja de Ahorros	4,544,271	2,521,972	55.50%	2,520,392	1,580
3	Banistmo, S.A.	7,587,567	2,493,100	32.86%	2,492,885	215
4	Banco Nacional de Panamá	6,866,390	2,236,996	32.58%	2,232,854	4,142
5	Global Bank Corporation	5,959,033	2,098,097	35.21%	1,951,228	146,869
6	The Bank Of Nova Scotia	3,034,514	1,190,325	39.23%	1,160,666	29,659
7	Banesco (Panamá), S.A.	2,644,738	1,066,696	40.33%	957,476	109,220
8	BAC International Bank Inc.	4,336,770	1,024,731	23.63%	863,243	161,488
9	Multibank Inc.	3,360,228	813,721	24.22%	812,596	1,124
10	Banco Aliado, S.A.	1,775,968	583,176	32.84%	153,303	429,873
11	Banco La Hipotecaria, S.A.	592,110	476,803	80.53%	476,803	-
12	Credicorp Bank, S.A.	1,282,959	359,940	28.06%	348,001	11,940
13	Mercantil Banco, S.A.	1,817,570	256,856	14.13%	252,020	4,835
14	Towerbank International. Inc	433,946	209,667	48.32%	128,609	81,057
15	Banco Davivienda (Panamá), S.A.	551,850	164,383	29.79%	137,640	26,743
16	Metrobank, S.A.	746,535	115,830	15.52%	77,361	38,469
17	Bi-Bank, S.A.	474,661	60,443	12.73%	12,390	48,054
18	Banco Lafise Panamá, S.A.	186,138	55,169	29.64%	49,982	5,188
19	Unibank, S.A.	374,800	54,297	14.49%	27,893	26,404
20	St. Georges Bank & Company, Inc.	453,353	36,524	8.06%	36,521	3
21	Banco Prival, S.A.	186,118	28,662	15.40%	28,662	-
22	Bancolombia, S.A.	127,781	27,781	21.74%	-	27,781
23	Canal Bank S.A.	341,502	27,583	8.08%	12,685	14,898
24	Banisi, S.A.	412,215	27,425	6.65%	27,425	-
25	MMG Bank Corporation	99,300	25,064	25.24%	11,692	13,372
26	Banco Delta, S.A.	200,797	18,994	9.46%	18,696	298
27	BCT Bank International, S.A.	328,690	16,987	5.17%	8,789	8,198
28	Mega International Commercial Bank Co. Ltd.	145,726	16,658	11.43%	1,734	14,924
29	Bank of China Limited	163,256	7,642	4.68%	4,802	2,840
30	KEB Hana Bank	70,038	5,678	8.11%	1,849	3,830
31	Banco Internacional de Costa Rica, S.A.	226,672	3,854	1.70%	2,782	1,072
32	Albank Corp.	32,032	3,234	10.10%	3,234	-
	Total	59,907,092	20,483,135		19,143,606	1,339,529

https://www.superbancos.gob.pa/estadisticas-financieras/cartera-credito

The previous table shows official figures shared by the Superintendency of Banks of Panama, in the Statistical Reports section for the year 2023.

The high percentage that mortgage loans represent of the total loans in general granted by the first five banks on the list is interesting. This may suggest that these credit institutions focus a good part of their market and customer service efforts on mortgage loans, which is why they are expected to be highly competitive.

It should be noted that mortgage loans not only contemplate the acquisition of a home, but also construction, remodeling, and refinancing. Each situation is described below:

• Housing acquisition: requested for the purchase of a new or used housing solution. A percentage of the price of the real estate is financed and the outstanding balance must be covered by the borrower.

• Construction: serves to finance the construction of real estate. It can be a home or commercial premises. The bank delivers the funds progressively as the construction project progresses, as previously agreed with the borrower.

- Remodeling: Used to make improvements or renovations to an existing property. The funds awarded can be used for expansion projects, repairs, updates, among others.

- Refinancing: Allows owners of existing homes or commercial properties to obtain a new mortgage loan with more favorable terms, whether a more favorable interest rate or longer payment terms.

5.2. Bank requirements to apply for mortgage loans.

In Panama, the requirements to apply for a mortgage loan from a bank or credit institution do not vary much from one another. However, each entity is free to apply its own rules, depending on the credit policies it has established. These policies can be conservative, liberal or mixed.

The requirements they ask for basically correspond to the following:

Salaried employee:

- Current job letter, with at least 1-2 years in the same place, with job continuity.
- Last pay stub
- Social Security record
- Valid identity card.

Independents:

- Valid identity card.
- Last two years income tax statement.
- Payment receipts for income tax statement submitted.
- Income tax good standing certificates.

The conditions granted in a mortgage loan may vary in the percentage of financing, time granted and percentage of interest rates.

5.3. Prime interest rates and other interest rates

As reviewed in Chapter 3, the new preferential interest rates for loans to finance first-time homes, whether for nationals or foreign permanent residents:

Preferential Rate Tranche No. 1 establishes a maximum subsidized rate of 5.0%, for a non-renewable term of eight years, for preferential mortgage loans for the purchase of new homes, with a purchase price of up to $50,000.00 at the time of financing.

Preferential Rate Tranche No. 2 establishes a maximum subsidized rate of 4.5%, for a non-renewable term of seven years, for preferential mortgage loans for the purchase of new homes, with a purchase price of $50,000.00 at the time of financing.

Meanwhile, Preferential Tranche No. 3 creates a maximum subsidized rate of 4.0%, for a non-renewable five-year term, for preferential mortgage loans for the purchase of new homes, with a purchase price at the time of financing of $80,000.1 cent, and up to $120,000.

5.4. Growth of the mortgage loan portfolio of Panamanian banks

The development of the real estate sector in Panama has been extraordinary. This is expressed in a news article published in "La Estrella de Panama", below:

"The mortgage loan portfolio for the purchase of the first home has experienced significant growth. The loans granted increased from $1,467.5 million in 2005 to $8,358 million in 2023. Although the total mortgage portfolio represents $17,500 million."

https://www.laestrella.com.pa/economia/sbp-anuncia-aumento-tasa-interes-FELE494919

It is interesting to appreciate how the construction sector in properties for private use, has immensely increased in such a way that it represents an important contribution to the Panamanian national GDP (10% estimated).

CHAPTER 6

Choosing your first home (what to consider?)

6.1. As a single person

Owning your own home is the main personal investment that every person should aspire to. Despite what some investors may say, a home is always an investment if it is made at the right time and with the right conditions.

It is important to balance individual priorities and needs. It is an advantage to do this while single since everything is more expeditious. It is important to evaluate location, size, and style of the home. Being single gives you the freedom to adapt your home to your personal preferences.

You should explore locations, neighborhoods, see first-hand what is nearby, whether shopping malls, hospitals, banks, parks, if they are centrally located, if they are to your personal taste and if it is within the contemplated budget. The important thing is that it reflects your personal lifestyle and includes favorite activities.

The decision to acquire a first home must be made with the vision of potential growth, and how this first investment can contribute to long-term plans on a personal and financial level. You must have an open, flexible mentality, be versatile, have the vision that the property can be adapted to different uses, not only as a home, but also as a workplace, which was established after the Covid19 pandemic, and that it be comfortable enough to be, if required, whether due to illness, unemployment or other reason.

For a single person who is starting out in the world of work, whether as an independent or salaried employee, it is very important to become a credit subject, so that they can obtain a mortgage loan at the best possible rate and time. In Panama, there is the concept of "first home" or "main home", which has a government subsidy at the rate or interest of the mortgage loan, and which allows any natural person to apply for a decent home.

Many times, you wait until you are in a relationship to consider the idea of purchasing your own home. Often, that partner does not arrive when expected and time passes. With this, valuable time is lost, and, in addition, space is taken up in credit capacity, with so-called bad debts, or credit cards. The best recommendation that can be given is not to wait to be in a relationship to acquire a first home. If later, that couple arrives, the home can be sold and the amount paid on the loan will be reimbursed and you once again could acquire another new home as a couple. Seen from a practical sense, it is advisable to take advantage of the favorable conditions that credit institutions and the real estate market have, not waiting to have a partner to take the leap.

However, mortgage loan rates are currently at their highest point in Panama in more than 20 years. Likewise, the prices of new homes are not as affordable and increasingly they are distant from the most convenient locations.

A first home must have the following minimum characteristics:

a. Environment and location: where it is located, if the neighborhood is safe, centrally located, are there facilities such as banks, schools and hospitals nearby. All this affects the valuation in the first instance.

b. Construction: it is key that the materials, finish and structure are in good condition. If the project is being planned, an interview must be held with those responsible to ask all the questions and have their answers and other details written down. The construction guarantee, in the case of a new project, is essential.

c. Supply and demand: is the real estate market in favor or against buyers? In Panama, demand remains high, and supply also exists, however, in the most desired or best valued locations and neighborhoods, prices are above USD180,000.00, which is the maximum value to apply for prime rates.

d. Economic news of the region or country: currently, Panama is going through, like the rest of the world, high interest rates on mortgage loans (inflationary economies), changes in the requirements for granting mortgage loans, high costs in construction industry (labor and materials).

6.2. As a married, in free union

As a couple, clear and timely communication is key in any project. It is important that both parties are clear about each other's expectations, desires, and tastes. A list of common points should be made that will help make the search for the first home together more realistic and suitable for both.

Everything that leads to obtaining housing must be done jointly, so that there are no misunderstandings and that there is always clarity. Doing it this way will strengthen the bond and build trust.

As a couple, you should especially plan for the long term. It is important that the goals are well defined and that the home to be acquired together evolves along with the relationship. Whether you are contemplating having children, expanding the home with annexes, not everything that is contemplated necessarily must be built immediately.

It is important that in negotiations as a couple, there is equity or at least the concessions of both parties have been made clear, so that later, there are no claims.

6.3. Investment (rent)

Real estate has traditionally been a haven to invest in, driven by a relatively stable economy, low inflation, strong currencies and sustainable economic growth.

Having rented real estate means a fixed monthly income and at a time when interest rates for savings accounts, fixed terms, high unemployment rates, are in unattractive terms, earning between 7% and 12% is an attractive option.

However, it is important to consider that real estate requires periodic reinvestment, covering maintenance fees to maintain its value. Likewise, if a sale is required, recovering its value and gaining profitability will depend on the moment in which the market is, what we know as a "buyers' market" or "sellers' market." These types of investments must be weighed, and their pros and cons reviewed, all focused on always improving financial health.

If the rented home has a mortgage, the rent amount must cover the costs of mortgage, maintenance, life and fire insurance, water supply service, and the garbage fee. The residual amount should be a minimum of 5-7% and kept in an account to be used as an amount for reinvestment (repairs, purchase of furniture in case it is rented furnished, or any other setback)

6.4. Doing numbers!

Before acquiring properties to rent, it is important to be clear about the profitability it will generate and its sustainability:

Profitability = monthly rent − monthly fixed expenses / monthly rent

Example: US$1400 monthly rent − US$1223 monthly fixed expenses / US$1400 monthly rent

= US$177 / US$1400
= 12.6% monthly profitability

Even having a good rate of return, it is important to consider the following points:

- The structural conditions of the property must be as optimal as possible. Require almost no investment. Except for the expected ones such as cleaning, painting, changing a ceiling lamp, as some examples.
- Location can never be overlooked. The more central it is, the more demand it will have, and the rental price will not decrease or will decrease very little, if not it will increase with a stable and/or growing economy.
- Define a healthy profile of tenants to guarantee, as best as possible, compliance with monthly payments and without delays. If the property is unoccupied, it is important that you have the funds to cover fixed monthly expenses for at least two months.

- The economic variables that directly affect demand must be considered, such as the unemployment rate, inflation, supply and rental prices. Taking these variables into account, it should give us a good perspective of the viability of renting the real estate, covering its fixed costs and obtaining a minimum profitability percentage.

Whatever the case may be, when investing in real estate for rent, you must have a reinvestment fund to keep the property in good condition to avoid lost its attractiveness for renting. A reasonable minimum amount could be, for example, three times the amount requested as rent.

CHAPTER 7

I have a property and now what?

7.1. Protect your investment

7.1.1. Annual maintenance

The structural maintenance of real estate is a fundamental part of preserving the value of the investment. The expenses to consider may vary depending on the type of property you have. If it is an apartment, the monthly maintenance fee and an amount for painting and minor repairs inherent to wear and tear over time, or known as conservation repairs, must be considered.

On the other hand, if it is a house, if there is no administration that includes maintenance, this expense must be planned, depositing a monthly sum in a savings account, which is no less than 10% of the rental amount, to have it as a reserve to meet the costs of conservation repairs such as roof repairs, exterior painting, and other expected repairs.

7.1.2. Location appreciation

The location of the real estate, in a stable economy with a strong currency, over time, it is expected to appreciate, even more so the locations with highest demand for being central and having a good level of quality of life. To be considered to have an environment with a good level of quality of life, it must have low crime rates, parks, banks, hospitals, pharmacies, restaurants, cafes, bakeries, as examples of convenience stores.

From the above, we can conclude that what increases the value of a property is:

- The first and most important thing is the location, depending on it, you could even have increases of double its value. Whether this becomes effective will fundamentally depend on supply and demand. If it is a location that continually increases demand and supply does not grow, undoubtedly the possibility of finding a home could even become an auction.
- With the Covid19 pandemic, having an attractive view, having terraces and balconies, can be a decisive differentiator.

- The age of the property, its conservation and the taxes status, constitute highly important factors to consider.
- That it is easily accessible, in addition to being interconnected with the main roads. With the construction of the metro, the proximity to the different stations increases the value of the property, as well.

Below, we list the main locations (names are in Spanish) with the highest demand in Panama City, for clients with medium-high and high purchasing power:

- Costa del Este:

This community is made up mostly of relatively new projects and is one of the locations with the highest demand and greatest appreciation in recent years. The square meter can be between US$2500 and US$3200. This neighborhood has an international hospital, restaurants, pharmacies, multinational companies, a shopping center widely equipped with all kinds of convenient businesses.

- Santa Maria:

This location, close to Costa del Este, is also one of the most valued and exclusive locations in Panama, its price per square meter can start from US$3000, at least. It could be assured that it is the most exclusive location in Panama, since it has a golf club and residences, unique amenities and luxury details. It is listed as one of the most expensive neighborhoods in Latin America.

- Punta Paitilla and Punta Pacifica:

These two urbanizations are among the best due to their privileged location, close to the Cinta Costera or Avenida Balboa, their buildings have the possibility of having views of the sea, Casco Viejo and Amador. They are centrally located, having in their surroundings the most luxurious shopping center in Central America and the Caribbean, the well-known Multiplaza Shopping Center. Likewise, the recently built Pacific Center.

The square meter ranges between US$2000 to US$3000 per square meter and varies depending on the age, views and amenities.

- San Francisco:

The zone of San Francisco, with high real estate demand, has traditionally been the location with perpetual demand, due to its incessant commercial activity. The square meter can range from US$1,500 to US$2,800 and will depend on its proximity to facilities such as Parque Omar, the age of the building, and whether it has a terrace or balcony. However, the Coco del Mar sector stands out, where luxury buildings have been built in recent years, so the minimum cost per square meter could be US$2000.

- El Cangrejo:

The famous and traditional Cangrejo neighborhood is a more open and popular area due to its offer of commercial premises conducive to nightlife, such as its restaurants, cafes and bars.

Via Argentina is in this neighborhood and a metro station. Due to its popularity, there is a wide variety of residential projects, both old and new, due to this its price per square meter is between US$1900 and US$2700. Again, it all depends on the age and amenities each building has.

- Balboa Avenue or Cinta Costera:

Just by having sea view, properties in this sector have a premium valuation. Additionally, close to the Cinta Costera, it is not surprising that the market value also increases. In this sector, there are also shopping centers, restaurants, pharmacies, hardware stores, supermarkets and everything convenient to have an excellent quality of life.

The price per square meter can range between US$2000 to US$3500, depending on the age and quality of the construction.

- Casco Viejo:

The neighborhood of Casco Viejo or San Felipe, as it is also known, is the historic center of Panama City and the most visited place by nationals and foreigners, for its attractive offer of bars, restaurants, hotels, old churches of colonial time. It was also declared world heritage by UNESCO.

In this neighborhood there are both apartments and houses restored and enabled to reside, all following and respecting the original construction line and in harmony with the rest of the complex. However, there is coexistence with residential areas that have not been restored.

In contrast, some important buildings were restored and converted into first-class hotels, the area is a beautiful example of colonial architecture adorned by vibrant urban art.

The price to live per square meter can range between US$2500 to US$3500

- Marbella:

A zone of residential buildings of a certain age and large spaces, as well as buildings with few years of construction. It is located around Balboa Avenue, it has cafes, bars and international restaurants that offer a dazzling atmosphere and extensive views of the sea.

In addition, it is located near the Cinta Costera, next to the sea, which every day has people exercising at all hours, walking, running, bicycling, among the most popular activities.

The price per square meter in this neighborhood could be between US$1800 to US$2500.

- Coco del Mar:

It is a neighborhood widely recognized for its natural beauty in Panama City that is located within the township of San Francisco, very central and close to places of interest such as the Atlapa Convention Center, Multiplaza Mall, restaurants, banks, private high schools, with excellent connectivity to the "corredor del sur", which easily connects with the banking center, Costa del Este and the Tocumen Airport.

The square meter in this neighborhood has increased in recent years, due to the construction of new and exclusive buildings that have first-class amenities. It could be between US$2000 to US$3500.

With reference to locations a little further away from the city center, but that still maintain a growing demand, we can mention: "12 de Octubre, Bethania, El Dorado, Albrook, Amador, Clayton, Howard". To mention a few. In these locations you can find different price ranges per square meter, everything will depend on the analysis of the property. However, they are locations that maintain good development of their surroundings and maintain a proximity to the highly valued city center.

7.1.2. ¿Do improvements increase value?

Each improvement, extension, renovation will differentiate and add value to the property. The perceived value is influenced by the improvements that have been made to the property.

If the property is in a group of houses that were built at the same time under the same design, a potential client will recognize the differences that must be considered.

Whether you want to rent or sell your property, there are recommended improvements that increase the value of the property and will make it more attractive to clients. Among these improvements are the following:

a. Kitchen:

The kitchen is the center of the home, where members of a family gather to prepare and enjoy daily meals and those that are only prepared during festivities and special moments. This is why many times; the kitchen makes a difference.

If the client is a family, it is important that the size of the kitchen is balanced. For example, it is not logical to have a large kitchen if you only have one bedroom. If, on the other hand, the property has three bedrooms, but the kitchen is small, the possibilities of renting or selling will decrease. Although in these times where time is the most precious thing, not many people dedicate much time to cooking, so, in some cases, this space in the house is seen as something relative.

To help the feeling of space, you can renew the finishes, furniture, lighting and, if possible, expand the space by reorienting the furniture and its layout.

b. Bathrooms

It could be said that bathrooms occupy second place in importance or even have a very similar value to a kitchen with balanced space and good lighting. Illuminated bathrooms, good finishes and spaces in line with the rest of the property are very attractive.

As in the kitchen, it is necessary to have the bathrooms in good condition and presentation. It is always advisable to have neutral finishes and colors, people have different tastes, and this will prevent it from being a reason for exclusion at the time of purchase or rental.

An attractive property for the market will be one that is in balance with the number of bathrooms and bedrooms it has. For example:

1 bedroom	1 full bathroom, half bathroom for visits
2 bedrooms	2 full bathrooms
3 bedrooms	2 full bathrooms, half bathroom for visits

If the property does not have this recommended balance, if possible, consider incorporating an additional full bathroom or a guest bathroom.

c. Improvements on the facade

Anything that is not presentable and requires repair on the exterior of a property must be fixed to obtain the best perceived value. This can be paint, garden, grass, and fences, to mention the most common.

d. Floors

The floors are "the mirrors" of the house or apartment. It doesn't matter that it has been painted, that you have modern furniture and good quality finishes if you have a worn, cracked, opaque floor, with old tiles, in short, neglected. In some cases, and depending on its quality, it should be kept in mind that an apartment could even increase the value of the property in an appraisal.

e. Minor repairs

Repairs to leaky faucets, a lamp or fan that won't turn on, rusty doorknobs, dull or old paint should never be neglected.

Once attended to, these details make a better impression and raise the perceived value of the property.

7.1.3. Improve loan rates, shorten mortgage time.

Panama is influenced by the interest rates on mortgage loans in the United States of America. The banking system uses these rates as a "reference", however, always keep in mind that each bank is free to implement their own credit policies.

To improve the loan rate, you must be aware of the downward fluctuations reported by the US market in its loan interest rates. However, this is no guarantee that all banks will lower their rates. But you can request a reduction from the bank and quote with other banks to evaluate. It is suggested to do this exercise at mortgage loan fairs, since many banks, as a promotional strategy, grant more competitive rates to certain clients they consider valuable.

On the other hand, capital payments can always be made. Before making such payments, the credit institution must be asked for instructions so that the payment to extraordinary capital is correctly verified. The ideal is to do it as many times as possible, if it is monthly, it is even better. No matter how small the amount, if it is done over several years, this will help shorten the time in which the loan is paid off and with this, the interest paid on the loan will be less than the initial amount. That is, less will be paid to the bank for servicing the loan granted.

7.2. Invest in a second home.

Acquiring a second home can represent an increase in family assets. However, important points must be considered to ensure that it does indeed represent an investment and not a loss:

7.2.1. Use of the second home

A second home can be used as a vacation property, for example, if you love the mountains, beaches, countryside, you could find an ideal home to spend time disconnected from obligations and a stressful life.

When you are clear about the use that will be given to the new home, you can plan the financing method. For example, investment properties are more difficult to finance as lenders consider them higher risk. However, if you choose to have a property for vacation or a second home for work, the interest rate will be lower than the investment rate. Of course, this ideology may vary depending on each credit institution.

7.2.2. How will it be paid?

a. Bank mortgage loan

If you are national, it will be easier and faster for you to apply for a mortgage bank loan. If, in addition to being national, you have a stable job, good credit references and creditworthiness, loan approval is almost immediate.

In theory, for investment homes, banks have a mortgage interest rate, which is above that of a primary or vacation home. Therefore, it would be ideal to give a significant down payment for the value of the property. The main mortgage banks should be contacted to compare conditions and rates, to make the best possible transaction.

However, whether you reside abroad or in Panama, but your income comes from abroad, you may need to better analyze your status to be eligible for credit. Some banks can finance the purchase of a home for investment, if you have a history or track record as a customer with the bank, such as a couple of years, if you are a permanent resident (not being national), or if you have worked in your country current employment for the minimum number of years required by the bank.

If you are approved for the loan, you may be asked for a down payment of 40% of the purchase price. But you must have quotes from the main banks that offer loans for investment homes; this percentage could be lower in several banks. The rate could be a minimum of 7% and a loan amortization period usually of 20 years.

It is noted that the above may vary or change depending on the credit institution being considered and without prior notice. Banks' credit policies are constantly reviewed and updated and will depend on the economic situation being experienced both locally and internationally.

    b. Loan with the Promoter

It is another financing option available in Panama to acquire a home, in this case an investment.

Each promoter will have their own requirements; however, they will be very similar to those requested by a bank. Developers do not offer long repayment periods, and the rate is usually higher than that of a bank, but it is a way to acquire a home, in case the traditional way of financing with a bank is not affordable.

c. Direct with the Seller

In Panama, it is very little known that a direct transaction is carried out with the seller, in terms of financing.

If it occurs, the negotiation would be carried out taking current bank interest rates as a reference, however, with much shorter amortization periods. This could be an option for a buyer who has good financial capacity but who does not want to make an immediate outlay for the entire price of the property.

This is the most expensive and least recommended option; however, it represents an option, in case the others are not among the possible options for the buyer. However, it is all a matter of reaching an agreement, formalizing the agreed points in a contract, always with the assistance of a lawyer, preferably, to ensure that both duties and rights are balanced between the parties and there are no situations that may cause future problems.

7.2.3. Have a plan for the use of the home, when it is not being used.

It is recommended that a property that is acquired as an investment should be seen as a long-term investment with fixed expenses and no income. This does not mean loss of value, since if it is not being used, the property does not lose its value over time.

It must be remembered that a property, even if it is not used, if it was made a good purchase and in a location of increasing value, it does not stop gaining or appreciating its value. It is very important to always have a contingency fund of at least three to six months of expenses.

If possible, consider renting it to family, friends or acquaintances for short periods of time. This unforeseen income may represent contributions to a savings fund for unforeseen expenses or another purpose.

If this economic plan is not carried out, there could be an erroneous perception that the property constitutes a loss due to the expenses generated and almost zero income.

Many properties are sold hastily, without even having an appreciation of their original value, due to the "high costs" generated by their maintenance. Sometimes this transaction can even mean a financial loss.

7.2.4. Sharing property with another person, sharing benefits and responsibilities.

When it comes to investing, we can do it alone or with partners, or a partner. Whether it is a family member, friend or simply another person (it can be natural or corporate), it is advisable to evaluate the possibility of incorporating a counterparty into the equation, so that both responsibilities and benefits can be divided. All in order not to waste a real estate investment opportunity and always keeping the rules of the game clear for both parties.

Credit institutions consider more than one person as a credit subject, if they have the capacity and good credit references.

This formula can work very well if the rules are well defined and respected by the parties.

7.2.5. Use your home as leverage to invest.

Panama's real estate market has appreciated significantly in recent years. Different elements have contributed to the appreciation of housing values, such as the cost of construction inputs, labor, oil prices, inflation, high demand and small supply in locations considered highly valued due to the quality of life that they offer.

If you have a home that can be refinanced, you can consider doing the exercise with your credit institution and see the possibility of receiving a sum of money to be reinvested in a business model that generates passive income.

7.3. Register your main home as family assets with the DGI ("Direcciòn General de Ingresos")

The home where you live with your family, or as a single person, benefits from a reduced rate of property taxes. If the requirements to apply are met and the registration of the property as a main home or family property is requested at the General Directorate of Revenue. The entire procedure can be carried out on the DGI website.

The requirements for exemption from the Property Tax for Tax Family Assets or Main Home are regulated in Law 66 of October 17, 2017, in Executive Decree 363 of December 4, 2018, and in Resolution 201-7078 of December 5, 2018. 2018.
https://dgi.mef.gob.pa/INM/PFT.php

Even in the case of being retired (55 years or older for women, 60 years or older for men, national or foreign) there is a "freezing of property taxes" which is nothing more than the payment of property taxes being not increased.

CHAPTER 8

I want to be a Real Estate Broker, Real Estate Agent, Property Manager, or whatever it's called!

8.1. Real Estate Broker License Requirements

The most widely known term for the profession of advising on the purchase and sale of real estate in Panama is "real estate broker", however, the term most likely to be used lately is "property manager"." or even "real estate agent."

The term is irrelevant, the most important thing is that you have the license to carry out said activity since in Panama it is a mandatory requirement. Panamanians and permanent residents in Panama for more than 5 years are eligible to obtain this license.

It is essential that as a professional in the real estate sector, you know all the regulations, laws, and everything related to the industry so that the profession is carried out properly.

To obtain the license, it is necessary to know all the relevant laws and regulations and thus be able to take the exam before the Real Estate Technical Board.

Below are the requirements for applying for a license at the Real Estate Technical Board at the Ministry of Commerce and Industries (MICI):

8.1.1. Natural Person Requirements:

https://mici.gob.pa/jtbr-requisitos-persona-natural/

1. Power of Attorney duly authenticated before a Notary.
2. Application on legal paper (stamped) submitted through attorney.
3. Guarantee bond of Ten Thousand balboas (USD) (B/. 10,000.00) in favor of the Real Estate Technical Board of the Ministry of Commerce and Industries.
4. Authenticated copy of the personal identity card issued by the Identification Directorate.
5. Immigration Status issued by the National Immigration Service stating that the person has been a permanent resident of the Republic of Panama for more than five (5) years (Foreigners only).
6. A printed passport size photo.

7. A passport size photo, sent to the email carnebienesraices@mici.gob.pa in JPG format.
8. Three balboas (B/.3.00 or USD) paid at the office of the Real Estate Technical Board, for the preparation of the card.
9. Twenty-five balboas (B/.25.00 or USD) in stamps by DGI ticket.
10. Record Police officer of the applicant.
11. Certification of passing the exam with its respective grade.
12. Copy of ID and suitability of the lawyer.

8.1.2. Legal Entity Requirements:

https://mici.gob.pa/jtbr-requisitos-persona-juridica/

1. Power of Attorney duly authenticated by a Notary.
2. Application on legal paper (stamped) submitted through attorney.
3. Bond that has coverage of Ten Thousand balboas (B/. 10,000.00 or USD) in favor of the Real Estate Technical Board of the Ministry of Commerce and Industries.
4. Authenticated copy of the Resolution, in which the real estate broker's License is granted to the president and legal representative.

5. Certificate from the Public Registry, which certifies the legal existence of the company, its directors and dignitaries, validity and resident agent. Legal representation will only be exercised by the president (qualified broker) in his absence, only by whomever he designates if he has a valid license or, if not, only and exclusively by the president.
6. Twenty-five balboas (B/.25.00) in stamps by DGI ticket.
7. Police Record of all dignitaries and directors.
8. Copy of ID or passport (foreigners) of all dignitaries and directors.
9. Copy of ID and suitability of the lawyer.

8.2. To manage his license:

Contact the Real Estate Technical Board of the Ministry of Commerce and Industries

Telephones: 560-0600 or 560-0700 ext. 5736, bienraices@mici.gob.pa or bienraices2@mici.gob.pa

8.3. Legal Framework

Below are the laws that are responsible for regulating and ensuring that the practice of Real Estate brokers is carried out in a professional and ethical manner throughout the Republic:

https://mici.gob.pa/jtbr-marco-legal/

- Law Decree No. 6 of July 8, 1999
- Resolution No. 1 of March 6, 2001
- Executive Decree No. 39 of November 7, 2001
- Resolution No. 5 of May 7, 2004
- Resolution No. 6 of May 11, 2004
- Resolution No. 2 of July 25, 2001
- Law 42 of 2000

8.4. Registration for the Real Estate Broker License Exam

8.4.1. National Person (natural or legal)

- Full Name.
- Identity card number or identity document.
- Home address or residential.
- Email.
- Payment of B/ 20.00 (USD) in cash.
- You must appear at the offices for registration.

8.4.2. Foreign Person

- Full Name.
- Identity card number or identity document.
- Home address or Residential.
- Email.
- You must have been a Permanent Resident in the Republic of Panama for 5 Years.
- Payment of B/ 20.00 or USD in cash.

NOTE: You have 60 calendar days to submit all the requested documentation after receiving the certification of passing the exam.

8.5. Procedure for taking the exam

- The aspiring real estate broker must register for an exam at the offices of the Ministry of Commerce and Industries, in the Hours Monday to Friday from 8:00 am to 3:00 pm. (For the interior area of the country, you can do it at the MICI Provincial Directorates, located in the cities of: David, Santiago, and Penonome.
- Registration can be done directly by the interested party or sent to a person with a copy of their ID and

information such as: email, address and telephone number.
- The registration fee is Twenty balboas (B/.20.00 or USD).
- The exam shifts are: 10:00 am to 11:30 am, and from 1:00 pm to 2:30 pm
- Once the exam is completed, you will automatically obtain your result.
- If you approve it, you will be issued a certification on the third business day, which must provide the other requirements for the suitability process. The exam has a maximum duration of one hour and thirty minutes.
- Once the exam is passed, it is required to request the issuance of the Real Estate Broker Certification.

8.6. Requirements to obtain the Real Estate Certification.

- A letter addressed to the secretary of the Real Estate Technical Board indicating the type of certification required with a copy.
- The document is received at the offices of the Technical Board.

- The certification is made and delivered to the interested party.
- This procedure takes no later than 3 business days once submitted to the offices of the Technical Board.

8.7. Syllabus for the exam

Exam Syllabus for Real Estate Broker

8.7.1. Laws and regulations of the Real Estate Technical Board.

- Decree Law 6 of July 8, 1999 "Law that Regulates the profession of real estate broker", Gazette No. 23,837 of July 10, 1999.
- Executive Decree No. 39 of November 7, 2001 "Regulation of Decree Law 6", Gazette No. 24,434 of November 19, 2001
- Resolution No. 001 of March 6, 2001 "Internal Regulations of the Real Estate Technical Board.", Gazette No. 24,308 of May 24, 2001.
- Resolution No. 002 of July 25, 2001 "Code of Ethics of the Real Estate Broker.", Gazette No. 24,408 of October 12, 2001.

- Resolution No. 006 of May 11, 2004 "Procedure for processing complaints", Gazette No.25, 076 of June 21, 2004.
- Resolution No. 012 of September 7, 2005 "Establishes that every advertisement must have the license number of the Real Estate Broker", Gazette No.25, 398 of October 3, 2005.
- Resolution No. 395 of September 26, 2008 "Establishes the penalty for failing to comply with the Resolution No. 012 of September 7, 2005", Gazette No.26,324 of July 15, 2009.
- Resolution 369-2008, Official Gazette No 26,317 of July 6, 2009, on the card and its value.
- Resolution 161 -2013 Official Gazette N°27,455 of January 17, 2014. "Validity of the Exam"
- All this information can be downloaded from the website of the Real Estate Technical Board

https://bienesraices.mici.gob.pa
(Transparency/Legal Framework)

8.7.2. Prevention of money laundering:

- Law 23 of April 27, 2015 "Prevention of money laundering" Official Gazette 27768-B of April 27, 2015,
- Law 124 of January 7, 2020, that creates the Superintendency of Non-Financial Subjects and dictates other provisions
- Executive Decree 363 of 2015, which regulates Law 23 of 2015 published in the Official Gazette 27845-B of August 13, 2015.
- Resolution No. 001-015 Warning Signs and UAF ("Unidad de anàlisis financiero" or Financial analysis unit) Forms
- Resolution No. 001-2016 By which non-financial reporting entities must adopt the warning sign guides
- Resolution No. 002-2016 By which non-financial reporting entities must adopt the Definitive Affidavit and Semiannual Affidavit forms.
- Resolution No. I-REG-001-17 Guide regarding compliance with prevention mechanisms
- Resolution I-REG-002-017 Guide for the effective application of current legal regulations
- Resolution No. I-REG-003-017 By which the Extra Situ form is established

- Resolution No. S-002-2021 of July 2, 2021, by which guides and procedures are issued to guide the SONF in the examination of unusual operations and the reporting of suspicious operations, related to the BC/FT/FPADM
- Resolution S-010-2021 of December 2, 2021 "Procedure to comply with the registration obligation of non-financial reporting entities."
- All this information can be downloaded from the website of the Superintendency of Non-Financial Subjects https://ssnf.gob.pa/ (Legal Framework).

8.7.3. Contracts

- Leasing (For contract drafts, contact MIVIOT, 4TH Floor Plaza Edison).
- Purchase Option
- Promise of Purchase and Sale
- Purchase and Sale contract
- Mortgages and Antichresis
- Brokerage
- These definitions can be found in the civil code, except for Brokerage (Commercial Code).

8.7.4. Lease

- Law 93 of October 4, 1973, on Leasing, published in the Official Gazette 17456 of October 22, 1973.
- Law 259 of December 2, 2021, Amends Law 93 of 1973 Leasing.
- Law 98 of October 4, 1973, published in the Official Gazette 17456 of October 22, 1973.
- Decree 37 of May 15, 1974, published in the Official Gazette 17597 of May 21, 1974.
- Law 259 of December 2, 2021 "Modifies article 13 of Law 93 of 1973" published in the Official Gazette 29427 of December 2, 2021.

8.7.5. Urban Planning and Zoning

- Law No. 6 of February 1, 2006, "That regulates Territorial Planning" published in Gazette No. 25,478 of February 3, 2006
- Executive Decree No.23 of May 16, 2007, Published in Official Gazette No.25,794.
- Law 9 of January 25, 1973
- Resolution 169-2004 of October 8, 2004, Official Gazette No 25,158 of October 14, 2004.

- Executive Decree 150 of June 2020 That repeals Executive Decree 36 of August 31, 1998, and updates the Urban Planning and Subdivision and Subdivision Regulations applicable throughout the national territory.

8.7.6. State and island lands/" Casco Antiguo" or old town

- Law No. 2 of January 7, 2006 "Regulates concessions for Tourist Investment and alienation of island territory for tourist purposes" published in Gazette No. 25,461 of January 11, 2006
- Executive Decree No. 85 published in Gazette No. 25,569 of June 19, 2006
- Law 80 of December 31, 2009, published in Official Gazette 26338-B, "Recognizes possessory rights and regulates titling in coastal areas and Insular Territory"
- Decree Law 9 of August 27, 1997, published in Gacetas No. 23,366 of August 30, 1997 Law of the Old Town
- Law 136 of December 31, 2013, Official Gazette 27455-A of January 17, 2014.

- Law 53 of July 4, 2017, Modifies and adds articles to Law 136 on Historical Monuments and Old Town

8.7.7. Taxes and Credit Banking

- Law 3 of May 20, 1985
- Law No. 4 of May 17, 1994, (FECI) Banks (preferential interest and its different tranches, complete information on residential and commercial mortgage loans, current market rates for loans residential and commercial mortgages) This information can be obtained at http://www.superbancos.gob.pa/
- Law 94 of September 20, 2019, that modifies Law 3 of May 20, 1985, that establishes the preferential interest regime in certain mortgage loans
- Executive Decree 29 of August 8, 1996, which regulates the FECI Law
- Executive Decree 554 of November 19, 2019, that regulates Law 3 of May 20, 1985, that establishes the Preferential Interest regime on mortgage loans and repeals Executive Decree 39 of June 3, 2009
- Law No. 66 of October 17, 2017 "Modifies articles of the Tax Code regarding Property Taxes as of

January 1, 2019" published in Official Gazette 28388-C of October 17, 2017.
- Law No. 28 of May 8, 2012. Calculation of the alienation tax 2% and gain 3%
- Law 255 of November 17, 2021, modifies Law 94 of 2019

8.7.8. Free Zones

- Free Zone Law. Decree Law No. 18 of June 17, 1948, published in Gazette No. 10,663 of June 28, 1948.
- Resolution JD-03-2009 of August 27, 2009, of the Board of Directors of the Colón Free Zone, through which new rental fees and rates for services provided are established. Official Gazette No. 26,358C of September 1, 2009
- Law 32 of April 5, 2011, "Which establishes a special, comprehensive and simplified regime for the establishment of Free Zones, Official Gazette 26757-B of April 5, 2011, updated by law 125 of 2013 Official Gazette 27,446 of December 31, 2011, 2013.
- Law 41 of 2004 "Panama" Pacific" published in Gazette 25103-A of July 28, 2004.

- Law 66 of December 13, 2018, that modifies and adds articles to Law 41 of 2004 that creates the special regime for establishment and operation in the Economic and Special Area called Panama Pacific and dictates other provisions.

8.7.9. Other Laws

- Law 80 of November 8, 2012. Incentive regulations for the promotion of tourist activity Official Gazette No 27,159-A of November 8, 2012
- Law 284 of February 14, 2022, Horizontal Property Law

8.8. Solving conflicts

The Real Estate Technical Board (JTBR) has, among other functions, the supervision and control of both companies dedicated to Real Estate brokerage and those people who independently carry out the profession. It has a Minutes and Correspondence secretary, who oversees the department.

The Real Estate Technical Board is created in the Ministry of Commerce and Industries and is under its supervision. This Board is made up of five members:

- The Minister of Commerce and Industries or the person he designates, who will preside over it.
- The Minister of Housing or the person he designates.
- The Minister of Economy and Finance or the person he designates.
- Two representatives, and their alternates, of the guilds or associations of real estate brokers with legal status, designated for a period of three years by the President of the country and chosen from shortlists presented by said guilds.

CHAPTER 9

Know and understand the profession.

9.1. The vocation of service and ethics.

Vocation according to the Royal Academy of Language (RAE) is an inclination towards a state, a profession or a career. Having a vocation for service would then be having the virtue of committing, with passion and a spirit of dedication towards an activity.

Having the vocation and being professional in it (that we practice, and that the activity is remunerated) would be the ideal state for anyone who makes a living in a specific job. In the specific case at hand, the profession of Real Estate Broker must also have the vocation, in addition to the profession as a state.

To obtain a housing facility for another human being, where they feel safe, sheltered and happy, produces satisfaction that goes beyond charging a commission for the service.

Services are intangible and have various components that will differentiate a good one from a bad one. When a service is provided, it will be characterized primarily by the treatment and management we have in human relationships, including colleagues, authorities, clients, service technicians and other human beings with whom they interact in the search for a home. either to rent or buy.

Professional ethics, on the other hand, refers to the set of norms and values that improve the development of activities in the profession.

Being ethical in the profession of real estate broker would include being reflective about what is understood as good conduct. That is, reflect rationally on your own behavior and environment in general. But, also think about the existence of your values, and deliberately choose the right thing and do the right thing.

There is nothing more that distinguishes a professional than his vocation for service and ethics.

9.2. Make yourself known.

As reviewed above, you can obtain a license as a natural person and as a legal entity. Each situation has its possibilities or options.

If you decide to obtain a Real Estate Broker license as a natural person, it is important to keep in mind that you respond in a personal capacity to any demand or complaint. Unless you are acting on behalf of a legal entity with its corresponding real estate license.

Once the operational figure has been identified, it is essential that the real estate services professional make themselves known by building their network or network of professional contacts, join a union, participate in all possible seminars and events related to the profession and maintain updated on related topics of interest.

As in any profession, a real estate agent or broker will create a reputation over time and its quality will depend on the vocation for service and ethics they have.

9.3. Work alone, with partners, or under international representation.

All options have pros and cons, let's mention the most obvious ones, however, each individual situation is different, so it is suggested that an objective balance be made focused on the personal goals you have as an entrepreneur.

9.3.1. Work individually:

- Pros:

Commissions are not shared, there are no misunderstandings with others, you work at your own pace, everything is more flexible and fluid since you do not have to agree with someone else to make decisions.

- Cons:

Operations may take longer than required since there is no one to help, even though decisions are made quickly and there is flexibility.

There is no deeper analysis or evaluation, since there is only one perspective of the situation. All expenses fall on a single economy. There is no economy of scale.

9.3.2. Work with partners:

- Pros:

There is an enrichment in the exchange of ideas and points of view on topics of interest to the business. Objectives and goals are pursued with an analysis enriched by feedback. The network is usually better in number and content, there are more opportunities to connect with a greater number of colleagues.

- Cons:

Possible disputes due to differences in opinions and course the business should take. Slowness in defining administrative policies, activities to be carried out and operations in general.

9.3.3. under a representation international

- Pros:

There is access to a properly organized database of properties to market, access to tools for proper conduct of activities, training in activities inherent to the profession, international name recognition, consequently, a better openness to the reception of services.

- Cons:

Commissions are lower, lack of flexibility in terms of procedures and other activities related to the profession.

Mandatory monthly sales level (not in all cases).

CHAPTER 10

Grow or stagnate in times of inflation!

10.1. About real estate bubbles and other demons.

A real estate bubble is created when there is an increase in the price of real estate without justified reasons, a situation that occurs when there is an imbalance between supply and demand. Since there is much more demand for properties, it cannot be completely satisfied, and the market takes advantage of it to raise prices.

Currently, investors begin to make profits by buying at low prices and then selling the properties for much higher prices.

In Panama there has been a lot of speculation as to whether there is a "real estate bubble", it is worth noting that we are talking about the real estate sector located in the towns or locations with the greatest demand to live, due to their advantageous environment and supply of housing.

It is speculated that in 2024 and at least the next two, the real estate bubble in Panama will burst or at least be "reinvented." This is because while it is true, real estate investors generally do not expect to see returns on their investment immediately, just as it is true that they are not willing to wait more than an acceptable period.

In Panama, the figure of rent with option to buy has existed for some time. This is nothing more than agreeing on a minimum rental period and at the end of this, paying the amounts paid in rent to the advance or initial payment to apply for bank financing.

In these times of high interest rates, which have no hope of falling, at least not in less than two years, according to experts, it is recommended to opt for rent with an option to buy, in the hope of waiting for interest rates to are more convenient and thus avoid incurring a very high financing cost.

10.2. Excess supply and demand restricted by high interest rates.

In 2024, interest rates for loans will remain high in the US or a minimum adjust will be done. This is what they have planned to maintain to combat the rampant inflation that the US economy was experiencing. Despite the good results in the first months of the North American economy, they have not yet wanted to adjust the rates, waiting for the political scenario, although they do not want to openly admit it.

Panamanian banks use US interest rates as a reference, just like European banks, although it is not recognized. Therefore, if they do not adjust downwards (latest forecast is September 2024), the Panamanian real estate market will not present major changes.

Likewise, the expectation is maintained of the revisions of subsidies for preferential interests for this year 2024, which coincides in dates with the inauguration of the new government, chaired by José Raúl Mulino of the "Realizando Metas" Party (RM).

Due to the above, the Panamanian real estate market is going through a significant stagnation or slowdown, also having other important factors that are added to it, such as inflation or decrease in purchasing power, and the unemployment rate that is estimated by the authorities at 7.4% but that in reality it is experienced much higher.

10.3. "Staying alive"

Surviving in a slow real estate market like the Panamanian market is not an easy task. However, these are moments where creativity becomes necessary, both on the part of real estate agents and credit agents.

High prices for labor, construction materials, unemployment, and high interest rates make it very difficult for the sale of new projects to move at the speed of previous years.

It is interesting then to consider that credit entities and owners of second-hand properties, built at lower costs, could agree on conditions that allow greater access to clients due to the assumption of having a better margin for negotiating prices.

In Panama, it can be deduced that there are several real estate markets "in parallel" in addition to the already identified "first-hand" or new real estate markets and "second-hand" or old real estate markets.

In the second-hand market, there are many properties that are "off the market" because they do not have the necessary characteristics to "qualify" to be part of the offer and that are attractive and have the required demand.

It would be interesting for real estate agents to identify these properties for potential investors and to enable these properties, buying at low prices and selling at competitive prices. This is the "flipping" service, which already exists, but is not widely spread in our country.

In short, it is key that the real estate market in Panama reinvents itself in an authentic and definitive way and opts for solutions designed "outside the box."

BIBLIOGRAPHY

- GDP growth projection for 2024 in some countries in Latin America, including Panama. ECLAC
- Growth of the gross domestic product of Panama 1990-1999. International Monetary Fund.
- National GDP and participation of the construction sector. National Institute of Statistics and Census, Comptroller General of the Republic of Panama.
- Superintendency of Banks of Panama.
- General Directorate of Revenue of Panama
- Ministry of Commerce and Industries of Panama
- Wikipedia, the free encyclopedia.
- National Assembly of Panama
- Presidency of the Republic of Panama

www.ingramcontent.com/pod-product-compliance
Lightning Source LLC
Chambersburg PA
CBHW070151230526
45471CB00002B/618